James Francis Tennant

Report on the total Eclipse of the Sun

James Francis Tennant

Report on the total Eclipse of the Sun

ISBN/EAN: 9783337052249

Printed in Europe, USA, Canada, Australia, Japan

Cover: Foto ©ninafisch / pixelio.de

More available books at **www.hansebooks.com**

REPORT

TOTAL ECLIPSE OF THE SUN,

AUGUST 17–18, 1868.

AS OBSERVED AT GUNTOOR, UNDER INSTRUCTIONS FROM

THE RIGHT HONOURABLE THE SECRETARY

OF STATE FOR INDIA.

BY

MAJOR J. F. TENNANT, R.E., F.R.S., F.R.A.S., F.M.S.

SUPERINTENDENT OF THE EXPEDITION.

(*Forming Part of Vol. XXXVII. of the Memoirs of the Royal Astronomical Society.*)

PRINTED BY STRANGEWAYS AND WALDEN,

CASTLE STREET, LEICESTER SQUARE.

PAPERS.

I. *Report on the Total Eclipse of the Sun, August* 17-18, 1868, *as observed at Guntoor, under Instructions from the Right Honourable the Secretary of State for India.* By Major J. F. TENNANT, R.E. F.R.A.S. F.M.S. Superintendent of the Expedition.

Read December 11, 1868.

Preface.

OBSERVATIONS of the total eclipse of August 17th, 1868, were deemed so important, that the Astronomer Royal, with the concurrence of the Council of the Royal Astronomical Society, addressed the Secretary of State for India on the subject, and recommended that preparation should be made. It was ultimately determined that the expense should be borne jointly by the Government of India and the Imperial Government, and I was appointed to superintend the operations.

The modes of observation were to be threefold :—

First. The spectroscope was to be used, to examine the Corona and prominences, as to their source of light.

Second. The polarization of the light of the Corona and prominences was to be examined.

Third. Several photographs were, if possible, to be taken in the absence of the Sun.

I had originally intended to superintend the photographic operations myself, employing soldiers of the Royal Engineers for the manipulation of

ROYAL ASTRON. SOC. VOL. XXXVII.   B

the plates; Lieutenant Herschel, R.E. was to have undertaken the spectroscopic examination; and Captain Branfill was to have had charge of the telescope for polarization. During the time that this scheme was under consideration, however, the Royal Society determined to supply instruments to Lieut.-Col. Walker, R.E. Superintendent of the Indian Trigonometrical Survey; and Lieutenant Herschel, who is attached to his Department, was selected for the superintendence of that Expedition. Under these circumstances, as I could hardly expect Colonel Walker to lend me a second officer (Captain Branfill being also a Member of his Department), I resolved to take charge of the spectroscope myself, leaving the management of the photography, during the total phase, to a non-commissioned officer of the Royal Engineers; I could thus insure that the baths, &c. were in working order, and give all necessary instructions. Sergeant Henry Phillips, R.E. was strongly recommended to me for, and appointed to, this duty.

The instruments intended for each class of observation will be described under its head, and I shall divide this Report as follows:—

1st. A narrative of my proceedings up to my return to Calcutta.

2nd. The astronomical determination of place.

3rd. The Sheepshanks' Equatoreal and the spectroscope observations made with it.

· 4th. The Astronomer Royal's telescope and the polarization observations.

5th. The silver-glass reflector and the photographic operations.

And I shall conclude by an examination of the results of comparing these observations together.

First.

A Narrative of Proceedings.

Up to the time of my leaving London, my proceedings have been reported, in a paper in the Supplemental Number of the Royal Astronomical Society's *Monthly Notices* for 1867; and in the Annual Address of the President in February 1868; it is now unnecessary to recur to them. I left England on January 12th, 1868; I reached Alexandria on the 18th, and embarked at Suez on the 19th for India; Aden was reached on the 25th January, and, as this was nearly the first place where observations of the totality could be made, I determined to use our short stay in endeavouring to secure some.

For this purpose I called on Captain Davis, Agent of the Peninsular and Oriental Company, to enlist his services; and at his house was fortunate enough to meet an old companion, Major Napier, of the Royal Artillery. Both these gentlemen promised their aid; and I learnt from them that Colonel Addison and Major Weir, of H.M.'s 2nd Queen's Royal Regiment, would be likely to be valuable coadjutors. It being then too late to look them up, I asked Major Napier to broach the subject, and promised to write as soon as I could. This I did, and it will save time if I say at once what my recommendations were. 1st. I recommended that they should endeavour to make drawings of the corona and appendages as accurately as possible, and urged that, if two observers were available, two sketches, made independently of the same part (say a quadrant) would be more valuable than single sketches of large portions which could not confirm and interpret each other. 2nd. I undertook to send, if wanted, a polariscope, and I did accordingly send one on Savart's principle, with instructions which I thought would be sufficient for its use. 3rd. I suggested that Colonel Addison should address Mr. Huggins as to getting a spectroscope for hand use, which he did with a favourable result. I hope, therefore, that there will be some results from Colonel Addison's observations.[*]

---

[*] Since writing the above I have heard from Colonel Addison, that clouds rendered their spectroscope and polariscope observations useless. He sends me, however, a sketch of the

To return to my own proceedings. I had arranged to stay at Madras during the interval between the two successive steamers calling there, in order to make inquiries about the advantages of the various places on the East Coast of India. The result was certainly depressing. It seemed that (contrary to my expectations) there was usually a considerable amount of rain on the East Coast in August about the parts where the central line crossed it. The register of Guntoor indeed showed but a few days of rain, but the amount seemed excessive, and the only encouragement was, that in no case did rain fall about the 18th of August.   It was confidently asserted, however, that the rain was that of the south-west monsoon ; this in my opinion was impossible, besides it did not cease at the usual time of the south-west monsoon's ceasing ; but it was alleged that the end of August being the wettest time the rains continued till the end of November.   The Bay of Bengal to the East seemed to me to be the true source of the rains, though the lower wind might not be easterly ; and I inferred that the rain would have a tendency to fall in the night and in the afternoon, for which opinion I found on close inquiry some confirmation ; and further that strong westerly winds would, while producing great rain in the west of India, clear off the clouds on the east coast.* My subsequent residence at Guntoor confirmed both these deductions, and it was often a curious sight to see light clouds passing to the west in an easterly upper current to return at night from the Hills with rain.   In every instance a rise of the barometer brought clouds and rain, and I had other evidence of the truth of my induction.

While at Madras I learnt also from Mr. Pogson that he had been informed by Col. Strachey, R.E., that there was a tract of exceptional dryness under the lee of the Western Ghauts, and I wrote in consequence to Mr. Chambers, Superintendent of the Colaba Meteorological Observatory (near Bombay), for information. This he very kindly gave me, so far as he could, but I could not see that the promise was better than at Guntoor. I left Madras on the 25th February and landed at Calcutta on the 29th.

protuberances, which shows that no material change took place in them in the interval between the totality at Aden and that at Guntoor; also some notes on the fleeting shadows and an account of the Austrian and Prussian doings.

  * This expectation has been completely verified, though the observers at the Western Stations did not generally lose their time.

On the 12th March, Sergeant Phillips and the two Sappers who were to assist him in manipulation arrived in Calcutta.

Up to this time I had heard nothing of the instruments, some of which were ready to start when I left England, and others on the point of being so. It was the end of March before anything arrived, and I then received the Astronomical Society's Sheepshanks' Telescope (afterwards described) and that lent me by the Astronomer Royal, each with their apparatus, and also the chemicals and photographic requisites. The cases were greatly injured and much of the glassware was broken. Both the telescopes had come safely, but some injury had been done in minor matters. Up to this time I had been selecting chronometers and instruments, and having them put in order; now the damage done to the new arrivals was taken in hand. My old friend Col. Thuillier, R.A. (the Surveyor General), had been instructed by the Government of India to aid me in every way, and he had placed the resources of his mathematical-instrument workshop at my disposal as far as urgent calls on it would admit. I am very greatly indebted both to him and to Col. Gastrell (under whose more immediate orders the workshops were) for the facilities I had. The result unfortunately was not perfect, but we had to content ourselves with apparent correctness, having no means, either in the cramped workshop or my temporary residence, of trying the instruments satisfactorily.

The Silver-glass only arrived early in May, and the cases were in a worse condition than those of the first instalment of instruments; indeed so bad was their state that the person sent to receive them refused to take delivery. It was the 15th May before terms were settled with the steam-agent and the cases placed where their contents could be readily examined. I had nearly given up all hopes of photography, but fortunately the damage was less than it appeared, and no small pieces were lost. After some alterations which will be spoken of in due course, this instrument, too, was repacked and I was ready to start early in June.

The rains of the south-west monsoon were now imminent on the West Coast of India,* and the rise of the rivers and bad quality of bye-roads

---

* When we crossed the Kistnah and the Godavery between Coconada and Guntoor, both were falling after floods, showing that heavy rain had fallen on the Western Ghauts, in which they rise.

consequent on rain had rendered it in my opinion impolitic to attempt, with my heavy baggage, to reach any Western Station, even had I felt sure that any decided advantage was to be gained by going there. The first steamer down the East Coast was on June 15th, and by that I and my photographers took our passage with all our apparatus. The last few days had been very wet; from the 6th June to the morning of the 15th, 21·3 inches of rain had been registered at the Surveyor General's offices and the veering wind showed that the centres of two circular gales had probably passed near Calcutta. Accordingly when we reached the mouth of the Hooghly on the 17th (it still raining) we were met by a heavy sea, and found that steamers which had left Calcutta two and three days before us were still lying there, waiting for the weather to moderate. We were fortunately able to get out to sea undetained, and after passing Point Palmyras had nearly clear sky and fine weather, reaching Coconada at seven P.M. on the 22nd June. Here the cases were sent to the mouth of the canal; transhipped into a barge under Sergeant Phillips' superintendence, and started off for Bezwada. I followed in a small steamer which had been placed at my disposal by the Superintending Engineer, and we all arrived safely at Bezwada on the 29th June. From this place it was necessary to proceed eighteen miles by land to Guntoor, where I at last found myself on July 3rd, with all my apparatus safe, except a mercurial barometer, whose cistern had become leaky from the extreme heat.

Mr Wilson, the sub-collector of Guntoor, had invited me to stay at his house; and finding the enclosure in which it stood apparently well adapted to my purposes, I, with his consent, made arrangements for building the pillars for my instruments. Shelter for the silver-glass had been, as soon as I had resolved that Guntoor must be my destination, ordered to be made at Bezwada, and when I was passing through, I added an order for a tent for the Sheepshanks' Telescope, under a promise that both should be sent me in a week. This was not fulfilled, and from one cause and another it came to July 20th before I was in a position to put either of the tents in place; I then found that so much alteration was absolutely necessary to fit the roofs, that it nearly amounted to a reconstruction of those parts. Meanwhile the strong westerly wind which had rendered the heat nearly intolerable to me from the day I landed at Coconada, had been replaced by alternating winds from the west and south, giving fine mornings, but cloudy afternoons, and rain in the evenings and at night. Eventually the west wind became very light, and we had a rarely broken grey sky, and frequent rain. Using what stray opportunities I found, I got the Sheepshanks' Telescope first, and then the silver-glass, into position before the rain cleared away entirely. August 8th was the first fine day, the wind having blown strongly from the west for three or four days, and gradually cleared away all the clouds. It now became hot and dry again, though by the 18th, it was showing symptoms of a change. The morning of the 18th was cloudy at daybreak, but these clouds soon cleared and we had every promise of a fine day. By 8 A.M. a wedge-shaped mass of light cumulo-stratus had formed to my east, having its vertex above the Sun, and extending later to the horizon. It covered the Sun till nearly ten minutes after totality and was very low, for Dr. Janssen, half a mile to the west of me, saw the Sun clear of it before the totality. I cannot help ascribing its existence to a sheet of water, forming the surface of a tank about half a mile from me ; especially, as when observing in the morning, I had frequently been troubled with clouds forming near the same part of the sky.

Soon after the 18th the weather broke, and we were much troubled with clouds, but having satisfied myself that the photographs were worth something, though not exactly what I had contemplated getting, we endeavoured first to secure them from harm. To this end six trans-parent positives were made from each, the diameter of the Moon being enlarged to 2½ inches, and a few negatives were taken still larger ; after these precautions we packed all up.

My heavy baggage left Guntoor in charge of Sergeant Phillips for Bezwada on the 2nd September; I followed on the 5th; we reached Coconada on the 9th, left it on the 17th, on the arrival of the steamer, and on the 23rd reached Calcutta with the instruments.

SECOND.

The Astronomical Determination of Place.

During my detention at Calcutta waiting for the first instalment of instruments, I had selected from the stores of the Mathematical Instrument Department two chronometers, DENT No. 2071, and BARRAUD No. 1659, a Repeating Circle by TROUGHTON, and a Mercurial Barometer, and these had to be put to rights.*

The chronometer DENT No. 2071 was a very old friend; it had been a sidereal chronometer, and a very fine one, and though it had been regulated to Mean Time by a local maker, it still seemed to go very well, temperature having but little effect on it. The other, a pocket chronometer, went apparently well, but the rate was very large. Knowing that a speedy adjustment of rate was out of question with any professional maker, I determined to reconvert the DENT to a sidereal chronometer, and to reduce the rate of the other; and this, perhaps hazardous, experiment succeeded. I found that I was liable to make mistakes with the BARRAUD when several observations had to be taken in quick succession, and gave up its regular use. When I wanted two chronometers it was employed; but it was compared by coincidence of beats with the DENT, before and after the observations, all times were thus converted into time by DENT, and then into sidereal time.

The following is a Table of the errors and rates of DENT during the time when it was retained in use for work. They were all determined from zenith distances with the Repeating Circle calculated with a latitude of 16° 17′ 29″·0 N. The refractions were computed from BESSEL's Table as given by CHAUVENET in Vol. II. of his *Practical Astronomy.* Two thermometers by NEGRETTI and ZAMBRA, whose errors had been determined at Kew, were employed for the temperature; and the Mercurial

---

* As a precaution in case the Repeating Circle should fail, I also borrowed a TROUGHTON's Circle, but it never was used.

Barometer having failed, as before mentioned, I employed an Aneroid by NEGRETTI and ZAMBRA which had been very carefully carried by myself. I had found its error on the reduced Barometer to be insensible, and its temperature correction the same. On return to Calcutta the correction to reduced Barometer was −0·04 inch.

Date.	Time by Dent.	Object Observed.	Correction to Sid. Time.	Rate.	Adopted Corrections.
July 17	h m s 4 27 5·08	Sun E	s − 7·03		
19	3 43 49·86	„ E	− 7·62	− 0·29	
20	16 21 15·63	α Aquilæ E	− 7·24		
24	17 52 13·37	α Boötis W	− 4·77	+ 0·60	
Aug. 1	16 44 54·67	α Aquilæ E	+ 3·66	+ 1·06	
7	16 28 31·23	α Aquilæ E	+ 9·47	+ 0·97	
8	23 17 36·07	α Aquilæ W	+11·01	+ 1·20	
9	18 0 21·38	α Boötis W	+11·21	+ 0·27	At 10ᵈ 0ʰ + t
11	1 19 2·50	α Tauri E	+12·84	+ 0·71	12ʰ·00 + 0ˢ·51 t
12	23 42 24·84	α Aquilæ W	+12·80	− 0·04	
13	0 10 31·69	α Tauri E	+15·29	..	Winding irregular
14	2 26 32·28	α Orionis E	+15·67	+ 0·35	At 17ᵈ 0ʰ + t
17	16 50 47·42	α Boötis W	+15·83	+ 0·06	15ʰ·75 − 0ˢ·321 t
20	1 3 5·74	α Tauri E	+13·63	− 0·65	− 0ˢ·092 tᵏ
23	1 53 22·55	α Orionis E	+13·55		

The Repeating Circle for Zenith Distances was by the late EDWARD TROUGHTON. It is so nearly similar to the instrument described in PEARSON's *Astronomy* that no detail seems necessary. During my stay in Calcutta I had a steel pin, removable at pleasure, applied for the purpose of fixing the plane of the vertical circle, instead of setting an index and clamping. This adjustment was more definite and firmer than the old one; which the small radius of the setting circle rendered defective. All the clamps were carefully examined and made to bite, and a small level was applied for the purpose of approximately adjusting the vertical axis. I also had five horizontal and the same number of vertical wires inserted, at intervals of about five minutes, intending to use the instrument as one for equal altitudes.

When I arrived at Coconada I availed myself of the short delay there to determine the value of the level scale, and, as Dr. Pearson does not give any description of this process, I may enter into some detail. A near* and well-defined object having been selected, and the vertical axis duly adjusted, ten repetitions of the zenith distance were taken, the bubble being in each case so adjusted that the end near the object-glass, or *object end*, read as much as possible higher than that next the observer, or *eye end*. The result was a zenith distance of 90° 11′ 42″·87 − 20·375 divisions of the level scale. Then ten repetitions were taken with the eye-end of the level kept at the higher reading; the resulting zenith distance being 90° 10′ 16″·12 + 19·715 divisions. Hence 40·090 divisions = 86″·75, or 1 division = 2″·164. This was early in the morning, when the temperature was low; later in the day, about the time of maximum temperature, the process was repeated with a more distant mark. I now got 38·24 divisions = 85″·62, which gave one division = 2″·239. This agreed so nearly with the previous value that I finally adopted 2″·2 the mean of them as the definite value of one division; and I have always used the following formula for correcting for the level error.

Let A be the initial reading, and B the final one; let m be the number of repetitions, involving p whole circumferences, and let ζ be the zenith distance (or the mean); also let ΣE be the sum of the readings of the eye end of the level, and ΣO the corresponding sum of the object end readings, then

$$n\zeta = B + 2p\pi - A + 1''\cdot1\,(\Sigma E - \Sigma O)$$

which is so easy to apply that no table of corrections is needed.

When I began using this instrument for astronomical purposes, I found that the results were perfectly wild. There were clouds nearly every evening, and (stars being often observed in the openings) the true star was sometimes mistaken; but even in cases where there was no possibility

---

* It was necessary to have a *near* object on account of the change of altitude from terrestrial refraction between the two series of observations; and also because anything distant became ill defined as the Sun rose and the atmosphere was heated.

of this, I could not reconcile results. I then found that the clamps were still imperfect and slipped, and that while the stops were of very little use with a moving object, the least touch of the arm intended to meet them, displaced the clamp. No care could entirely avoid this at night, so I entirely removed the arm, and set myself to acquire the habit of setting the telescope by the circle, when they were clamped together, instead of touching the parts more directly connected with it. My troubles now nearly vanished, and the more I used the instrument the more I liked it. Its great defect is top-heaviness, which renders it unstable. In these investigations into the source of my discrepancies, I also found that the chronometer Barraud, which had five beats in two seconds, was difficult to read quickly, partly from the number of beats, and partly from a small eccentricity of the axis of the second-hand on the dial; this was the reason of my discarding its habitual use.

The following are the results I obtained for latitude, in reducing which I used *Nautical Almanac* places for the stars where available, taking those of the others from the Greenwich Seven-year Catalogues, with Proper Motion from a comparison with the Twelve-year Catalogue.

				°	′	″
On July 18	By 10 observations	α Scorpii	16	17	29·7
19	10	„	ρ Draconis			29·6
19	10	„	Polaris			28·4
20	10	„	η Ophiuchi			12·0
Aug. 9	16	„	α Scorpii			24·7
13	8	„	α Cassiopeæ			29·2
14	14	„	δ Draconis			32·4

The result from η *Ophiuchi* is discordant, for which I can find no cause. I was prevented from repeating the observations, and have rejected them entirely. There is so large a number of observations of α *Scorpii* that its N.P.D. becomes of some importance. I have found that the equations given in Mr. Stone's examination of Bessel's Refractions (in Vol. XXVIII. No. 2, of the *Royal Astronomical Society's Notices*) would be better satisfied by assuming * R = true refraction = R_r [9·998704] − [8·0824] tan² ζ.

---

* If we follow the mode of adjusting discordances of N.P.D. adopted by Mr. Stone, we shall, it seems to me, be assigning a different index of refraction to air of the same density, at different places. In my hypothesis, if the coefficient of R_r be determined from the places

At 83°, of zenith distance which may be taken as the mean efficient value in these equations in producing the coefficient in tan ζ we have, as equivalent, the more convenient formula

$$R = R_\tau [9.998704] - R_\tau^2 [4.60991].$$

If the effect of this correction be applied to the N.P.D. of α *Scorpii* from the Greenwich Catalogues, we shall have 116° 8′ 9″·81 as its mean N.P.D. for 1868·0, whereas from the *Nautical Almanac* it is 116° 8′ 10″·83. The use of the former value would increase the latitude by *Antares* by 1″·02. None of the other stars would have sensible corrections from this source. We should then have the following values of latitude

			°	′	″
By 26 observations of		Antares	16	17	27·7 N.
8	,,	α Cassiopeæ			29·2
10	,,	ζ Draconis			29·6
14	,,	δ Draconis			32·4
10	,,	Polaris			28·4

of which values the mean is 16° 17′ 29″·46, or if we weight according to the numbers of observations, we have,

$$\text{N. lat.} = 16°\ 17′\ 29″·23.$$

I had prepared predictions of a considerable number of occultations from the data given in the American *Nautical Almanac*, intending to use them for the determination of longitude. Of these I was able to observe very few.

	h	m	s
From the Immersion of 33 Ceti on Aug. 8 I got	5	21	48·8 E.
Immersion of α Tauri, on Aug. 12			53·1
Emersion ,, ,, ,,			50·3
First contact of Eclipse, Aug. 17			43·9
Commencement of Total Phase, Aug. 17			45·3
Last Contact of Limbs, Aug. 17			51·2

of several Observatories, and that of R_τ^2 be supposed peculiar to each, we practically assume that Bessel's law needs a slight correction, depending on the constitution of the air at the place of observation. R_τ is the refraction of Bessell's *Tabulæ*.

The emersion of 33 *Ceti* was so close to the S. point of the Moon's limb as to be useless; and an immersion of ξ, *Libræ* has not been computed for want of a reliable place of the star. All these values are uncorrected for errors of the Moon's and star's places, but I have the necessary equations of condition.* Assuming the mean for each day to have an error mainly dependent on the tabular errors, we shall have the longitude of the Repeating Circle † 5ʰ 21ᵐ 49ˢ·1 E. from occultations. I also observed equal altitudes of the Moon and stars on such nights as were available, with the Repeating Circle used as an Equal-altitude instrument. The values for each night are as follows. They are uncorrected, of course, for errors of the Moon's and star's places, but I have the means of making requisite corrections.

				h	m	s
On July 24	4 comparisons with	γ Virginis gave		5	21	53·4 E.
Aug. 1	2	,,	τ Sagittarii			46·6
9	2	,,	α Arietis			43·3
11	2	,,	ζ Persei			53·3
13	3	,,	ζ Tauri			47·9
14	2	,,	γ Geminorum			45·5

whose mean is 5ʰ 21ᵐ 48ˢ·3. In each case where there are two comparisons, each is a complete transit over the five horizontal wires. The difference of position of the Repeating Circle and Equatoreals has been neglected throughout. Hence, giving the same weight to the observations of one day, however obtained, I have a mean longitude of

$$5^h\ 21^m\ 48^s\text{·}6\ \text{East.}$$

Captain Branfill did me the favour of connecting my station with the marks of the G. T. Survey, and the deduced result is for the Repeating Circle

N. latitude 16° 17′ 34″·3
E. longitude 5ʰ 21ᵐ 46ˢ·65

The former depends on an observed latitude at Calcutta, the latter has

* I am indebted to Mr. Stone for errors of the Moon's Tabular place during this period, but having left my papers in Calcutta I am unable to give corrected results. The general result would be to reduce the longitude some seconds. [June 23, 1869.]

† Neglecting the error caused by observing with the Equatoreal.

been reduced to what would have resulted from the use of the longitude of Madras given in the *Nautical Almanac* by the application of $-3'\ 1''\cdot8$ to the G. T. Survey value.

The neighbouring hills and the defective mass of the sea would produce discordances in the same direction as these.

THIRD.

The Sheepshanks' Equatoreal and the Spectroscopic Observations.

The instrument used for the observations with the spectroscope was the Royal Astronomical Society's Sheepshanks' Telescope, No. 3, of 4·6 inches aperture, and 5 feet focal strength, which had been lent to me for the purpose, as stated in the President's Address for 1868. Mr. COOKE had mounted it equatoreally, in his usual way, before it was transferred to me; but the instrument, in that state, could not be used in a latitude so low as that of Guntoor. The Council, therefore, in lending it to me, authorised the necessary changes in the attachment of the polar axis to the iron pillar, which, with some additions not used for the purposes of this paper, were made. The spectroscope was fitted to this, and the necessary counterpoise added.

When I came to put up this instrument and adjust it to the low latitude, I found that, on attaching the clock, the counterpoise weight prevented the reversal of the telescope, and that consequently only one side of the meridian could be examined for about three and a half hours of hour-angle unless the clock was removed. Beyond three and a half hours from the meridian, it became absolutely necessary to remove the clock. Thus the first contact of the Sun and Moon could not be observed on August 18 without removing the clock; which prevented the use of this telescope for observing it. Another trouble was, that any change in the eye-pieces deranged the equipoise of the instrument, which could only be restored by shifting the telescope in the collars holding it. With the micrometers and ordinary eye-pieces I could neglect this precaution, but with the change to or from the spectroscope it was impossible to do so, and this prevented the free use of the telescope, as I never liked to make this change except in daylight, and when one European, at least, was available to assist.

The spectroscope had originally been made by Messrs. Troughton and Simms for the Astronomer Royal's telescope, and had only a single prism of flint-glass. The slit was placed in the focus of an object-glass of short focus and considerable aperture, which made the rays issuing from it parallel. After passing through, and being dispersed by, the prism, they were viewed as usual by a small telescope, on whose object-glass they fell. To identify any ray, in the absence of a spectrum of comparison, a scale of equal parts was reduced by photography to a small size. This was illuminated by a swinging lamp, and the rays from it having been rendered parallel by an object-glass, were reflected from the surface of the prism up the small telescope. They thus became visible at the same time as the spectrum. An arrangement was also provided, by which two plates of metal, close to the jaws of the slit, could be simultaneously moved outwards and inwards by eccentric cams, so that the length of the slit and breadth of the spectrum could be adjusted with the touch of a finger. The width could likewise be adjusted by a screw which moved one of the jaws. No cylindrical lens was provided for viewing stellar spectra ; this proved a very serious want, for I soon found I could not stand the exposure to the Sun's rays, which was unavoidable when using the spectroscope on it. A trial on *Saturn* showed me a spectrum, but so narrow and fading so much at the ends, that I could not work on it. The only preparation I could make, therefore, for the Eclipse, was to accustom myself to find the adjustments of the slit quickly, and to experiment on illumination of the scale. Eventually, I disliked the illumination from the swinging lamp so much, that I gave it up, and substituted a common bull's eye lantern, which was fixed to a swinging frame fastened to one of the angles of the Observatory tent.

The iron pillar of the Equatoreal-stand rested on a stone 2 ft. 6 in. in diameter, forming the top of a brick pillar of the same diameter, and 4 feet deep, standing on compact gravel. The surface of the stone was level with that of the ground, and the whole instrument was enclosed in an octagonal tent, 10 feet in diameter, with a pyramidal roof, such as is described by the late Captain Jacob as having been used over the Lerebours' Equatoreal at

Madras.   When the instrument was not in use, a waterproof sheet protected it from the leakage which, in heavy rain, is almost unavoidable in a shelter of this sort.

The first attempt to adjust the finder showed me that I could in no way get its crosswires into the optical axis of the telescope, or even within the radius of the field of the most powerful eye-piece, without loosening it from the main tube.   The wires, however, were not readily seen without some slight illumination, and I hoped, when I changed them, it would all come right.   It did not do so however, and, of course, in this state I had no power of identifying the object in the jaws of the spectroscope.   Eventually, I interposed a thick pad of paper between the telescope tube and the supports of the finder, in order to make the necessary adjustment of the wires.   The slit of the spectroscope did not exactly pass through the axis of the telescope; but, as in this case, it was evident that the upper and lower limbs alone of the Moon would be of great importance, it was placed horizontally, and the wires adjusted to it some days before the eclipse. On the evening of August 17, I brought *Saturn* on to the cross-wires of the finder, and its spectrum was seen in the spectroscope, showing a satisfactory adjustment, and, as I hoped, stability.   Dr. JANSSEN had very kindly offered me the aid of the mechanic and tools he had brought with him; and I should have done much better if I had availed myself of his aid; but I had no precise knowledge of his means of helping, and, busy as I was, it never occurred to me at the time that he had probably just what I wanted.*

Before the Eclipse began on the morning of August 18th, I directed the telescope to the brightest part of the sky (the Sun being, for reasons before given, unattainable), and compared the solar lines with the scale divisions. Beginning at 19ʰ 42ᵐ, I read,—

Solar Line C†	256·3 Div.	Estimated strength	4
	240·5	,,	3
	239·2	,,	3

---

* A good assortment of tools, a mechanic, and materials, are very desirable in every way when one is so far from assistance; but, having had everything attended to, I had no known wants; and I found, on attempting to select, that to provide for the possible wants would far exceed the sum I was authorized to expend.

† B was within the field, but I could only see it with Sun-light.

D	238·5	Estimated strength	6
	219·2	„	1
	217·0	„	2
	215·3	„	2
E	214·2	„	4
	212·3	„	2
	⌈210·0	„	4
b	⎨208·2	„	3
	⌊208·0	„	3
	202·3	„	3
	199·1	„	2
	195·2	„	2
F	191·0	„	4

Here it was necessary to adjust the focus of telescope and scale.

Again	F	191·0	was the reading and continuing	
Solar Line		179·8	Estimated strength	3
		168·3	„	2
		163·7	„	2
		160·2	„	2
		159·6	„	2
	G	154·7	„	6
		151·8	„	4
		150·5	„	4
		149·2	„	3
		147·8 ⎫ 146·1 ⎭ a band		
		143·3	„	4
		142·8	„	3
		141·3	„	1
		140·8	„	2
		138·6	„	4

Altered focus when the same line read again,—

Solar Line	G	138·6	Estimated strength	4
		129·3	„	3
		128·0 ⎫ double each	„	2
		127·0 ⎭	„	2
		123·7	„	4

Solar Line	121·6	a band	
	120·6	a band	
	119·3	Estimated strength	3
	116·5	,,	4

Ended at 20ʰ 2ᵐ through light clouds.

The first contact of the limbs of the Sun and Moon was observed with the repeating circle at 6ʰ 1ᵐ 57ˢ·0 by Dent, = 6ʰ 2ᵐ 12ˢ·66 sidereal time. I then proceeded to take a few transits of the cusps over the horizontal wires, but I found the line joining these too nearly parallel to the wires to give results with which I was satisfied, so I gave it up. At 6ʰ 16ᵐ 52ˢ Dent, the Moon's limb bisected a large spot; at 7ʰ 0ᵐ 59ˢ·5 it bisected the first one of a group of spots; and at 7ʰ 7ᵐ 55ˢ·5 it passed over the centres of two smaller spots in the same group.* These last observations were made with the finder of the equatoreal.

As the obscuration proceeded I closed the entrance to my Observatory tent, and lighted my lamps, only taking a look-out once for a few minutes. My time was fully occupied with the driving-clock, which this day was very troublesome. I had carefully adjusted it to go mean time by a chronometer, and then retarded its rate to the proper amount by means of the appropriate screw. Hitherto I had never found setting in Right Ascension cause any change of rate which could not be readily adjusted; but of course I had never had occasion to follow accurately with the Spectroscope. Now, the slightest attempt to set the telescope had such an effect on the clock, that constant recurrence to the finder was absolutely necessary. The cross-wires of the finder, too, had become very slightly deranged in North Polar Distance, but I did not think them worth touching. Meanwhile Mr. Wilson, of the Madras Civil Service, who had kindly undertaken to write for me, took his seat with his back to the Sun, and we awaited the disappearance of the Solar disk.

Directly I saw the whole Moon in the finder I set the cross-wires immediately outside its upper limb. By the time I got to the spectroscope, the cloudy range, seen in the photographs, had vanished from the slit, and I saw a very faint continuous spectrum. Thinking that want of

---

See *post,* observations with the silver glass.

light prevented my seeing the bright lines, which I had fully expected to see in the lower strata of the corona, I opened the jaws of the slit, and repeatedly adjusted by the finder, but without effect. *What I saw was undoubtedly a continuous spectrum, and I saw no lines.** There may have been dark lines, of course, but with so faint a spectrum and the jaws of the slit wide apart, they might escape notice. I then searched for the remarkable horn, projecting apparently upwards from the Moon's limb. The disarrangement of the wire I have spoken of lost me some time ; suddenly, however, it burst into sight, a gloriously brilliant linear spectrum. I closed the jaws of the slit as fast as I could, and hastily cast my eyes over the field. One line in the red was so beautiful that it needed an effort to turn my attention to anything else; there was a line in the orange not so well defined, and one in the green which seemed multiple (it must be remembered that I had not time to adjust the jaws of the slit accurately, and that the brilliancy of these lines made them broader by irradiation) ; beyond, I saw a line just defined, which, as will be seen from the measures before given, must have been near to F, and still further off in the blue I saw a hazy light probably beyond G.

Adjusting the lamp I read the red line at 256 divisions, the next at 238, and the green one at 210. While I was endeavouring to make up my mind about the place of the next one, which was hazy, the Sun reappeared, and this spectrum faded from view. At 8ʰ 11ᵐ, sidereal time, I read the lines as follows:—

Solar line	C	255·6
„	D	237·6
„	E	213·3
„	b	208·6 estimated mean of the three lines.

Up to this time all the adjustments were untouched. The changes of focus of the telescope had not evidently disarranged the scale, which I had always found stable in its adjustment.

---

* In the instructions for Lieut. Herschel his attention was first drawn to the protuberances. I therefore had resolved to attend first to the corona, lest each of us should have only the same partial tale.

The red and yellow lines were evidently C and D, the reading of the green line coincides with that of the brightest line in b, instead of the mean of the three lines, which I read as a verification; the line near to F was in all probability F itself; E was certainly not seen by me. The line in the blue it is useless from my data to speculate upon, I must hope that some one else has identified it. The last contact was observed at 8^h 47^m 9^s by Dent, $= 8^h$ 47^m 24^s ·62 sidereal time.

Before passing to another subject I would allude to two defects of the spectroscope I employed. 1st. To prevent its projecting inconveniently from the telescope for which it was intended, a collimating lens of very short focus was used; this entailed a very narrow slit to get definition, and thus a loss of light. 2nd. The ordinary achromatic telescope is not adapted for viewing the dispersed rays. It ignores almost entirely the less luminous blue rays, and these are important to observe. My divided scale was well seen throughout (especially if the light were reflected from the back, or brass surface, of the mirror), but it is seen that I had twice to adjust focus, and still did not reach from C to H. I think that the flint and crown lenses might be ground to bring C and G together. There would, of course, be a considerable secondary spectrum, and this might be remedied by the known methods. Whatever the objection may be to them when tried on large object-glasses, I have no doubt that one, an inch and a half at the outside in diameter, could be well corrected, and the result would be an enormous improvement in cases where the spectroscope is required, as here, to have a large range of colour.

I have said nothing of my personal sensations, for they were ignored as far as may be; but I may mention that I did not feel cold. I had been told that I should do so, and, in consequence, provided a great-coat to put on, but both inside and outside the tent I felt quite comfortable without any coat. All I could feel was as though the freshness of early morning lasted longer than usual. I had closed out all view of the sky except near the Sun, which I should describe from the hurried glance I took, as a cloud scene shaded in lamp-black, and the same cold tone seemed to pervade the shadows in the tent.

FOURTH.

*Observations with the Astronomer Royal's Telescope and the
Polarization Apparatus.*

I am indebted to Colonel WALKER, Superintendent of the Indian Trigonometrical Survey, for the services of Captain BRANFILL of his Department. I had the most perfect confidence that an officer trained in that
school would be a good observer, and my expectations have been completely realised. The notes I have before me were written at three times,
and all somewhat hastily; I shall therefore venture to abstract and re-
arrange them, but they bear evidence, not only that the writer of them
saw many things to which his attention was not especially directed, and
noted them, but also that small phenomena impressed themselves so
accurately on his mind, that he saw during the total phase appearances,
which certainly neither of us expected, and whose explanation proves the
accuracy and freedom from bias of his mind.

The instrument used by Captain BRANFILL for these observations was
3¼ins. in aperture, and 5 feet in focal length, it was, indeed, one of the old
collimators of the Greenwich Transit Circle. Mr. SIMMS had provided
it with a parallactic mounting to enable it to follow a star with one
motion. The polar axis was supported at each end in an iron cradle,
which was fixed to a bed-plate by a central pulling screw, and two
pushing screws at each end. The inclination thus admitted of some
adjustment, while two antagonistic screws at the south end adjusted in
azimuth around the central point of the cradle, and fixed all. The
declination axis was at the upper end of the polar one (just outside the
cradle) and it carried the telescope at one end and a counterpoise at
the other. The stump of a tree was firmly planted in the ground, and
its upper end so cut off that the plane of section nearly passed through
the pole. To this inclined surface the bed-plate was bolted by four
coach-screws, and the polar axis having been approximately adjusted
by means of a spirit-level to the latitude, the azimuth was fixed by making

both telescope and declination axis horizontal (apparently), and then bringing an object known to be in the meridian into the centre of the field. The inclination of the polar axis being now adjusted again all was ready. The difficulty lay in getting an object in the meridian. This arrangement was quite efficient and steadier than many of more pretensions.

The Polariscope eye-piece was made by Mr. LADD for a smaller telescope which had been lent to me by the Astronomer Royal, and was adapted by Mr. SIMMS to the 5-foot, with which it had a magnifying power of about thirty. It was of RAMSDEN's construction, having a positive focus, and was contained inside an outer jacket into which it slipped till a wire came into focus; close to this wire was an opening in the jacket, through which perforated plates (similar to the WATERHOUSE diaphragms of photographic lenses) could be inserted in order to limit the field of view. Inclosing the whole eye-piece, and passing beyond it, the jacket carried at the eye-end a small piece of tube, into which fitted two cells carrying the prisms; between these prisms and the lens nearest to it, there traversed backwards and forwards a right-angled prism of ebony, having in it two holes, one plain, the other carrying the compound quartz plate of a SAVART's polariscope. In one of the prism cells is a NICOL's prism, in the other a Double-image prism and quartz plate. With the jacket everything turned in an adapter carrying an index; and there were rough graduations on the jacket to enable the position of the wire to be known.

There were thus four combinations of the slide and prisms, which could be rapidly changed one for another, and which showed the existence of polarized light by differing phenomena. I proceed to describe these shortly, and shall in the descriptions assume that the light is polarized. If polarized light be absent then the phenomena are so too.

1st. *The NICOL's prism and the plain aperture in the slide.* On turning round the jacket containing the eye-piece objects shining by polarized light would vary in brilliancy. They would be brightest when the plane of the wire was also that of polarization, and faintest at 90° from this position on either side. Any objects whose light was unpolarized would be unchanged and would guide in detecting changes of brilliancy.

2nd. *By a touch the plain hole in the slide could be changed for the other.* This combination forms Savart's test. Now the field would be seen striated with bands of colours crossing those objects shining with polarized light, and interrupted where there was none. In this case the central band, to which the wire served as an index, was white* when the plane of polarization and that of the wire coincided, that on each side was black passing into blue, and so on ; all the rest being bands of colour. Turning the whole jacket and its apparatus to 45° from the former place the bands almost vanish, and further on at 90° the white band had become black, and the order of colours changed ; and if the motion were reversed the same succession of phenomena appeared. By reading the graduation when the central band is most clearly white, an approximation is obtained to the plane of polarization; and by making the bands vanish on either side two positions equidistant from the true plane can be got with considerable accuracy.

3rd. *The double-image prism and its attached quartz plate alone;* that is, with the plain hole in the slide. One of the diaphragms was necessary ; of these the diameter of the largest was just what the prism converted into two distinct images. These were seen of complementary colours, one having a red, and the other a green tint, strong in proportion to the amount of polarized light. If there were a field containing objects some of which were seen by polarized and some by ordinary light, then the change of tint would not extend to the latter. One side of the prism cell was marked† and the corresponding side of the tube into which it fitted ; when duly placed the marked side of the prism gave the red, and the other the green image, when the wire was in the plane of polarization. At right angles to this position the colours interchanged, and intermediately one image became what I should call almost pure blue (in Lieut. Her-schel's instructions it is called a purple), and the other a yellow orange ; these intermediate positions are more accurately determined than the maxima of red and green respectively, but I think this combination better

* In my previous account I described this as black. It was so then, but the apparatus is rough, and in travelling its adjustments had altered. Taking out the compound plate to clean it I inadvertently changed its position, and as Captain Branfill liked the change I let it remain. Personally I prefer the previous arrangement.

† Captain Branfill devised very convenient arrangements for avoiding mistakes.

adapted to show the existence of polarized light, than to determine the plane of polarization.

4th. *When the compound quartz was slipped under*, each image became striped with alternate red and green bands ; the central one being red in the red image and green in the other. This was a delicate test of the existence of polarized light, and possessed the property of the second test, that at 45° from the plane the bands vanished, but at the same time the blue and orange tints of the last test became visible.

Of the four combinations I prefer the second for general use, but perhaps the fourth is better for some cases.

Captain BRANFILL arrived at Guntoor early in August, while it was wet and little could be done. He had brought one of the Observatory tents of the G. T. Survey with him, and under shelter of this, the instrument he was to use was put up; he then set to work to familiarize himself with the phenomena produced by polarized light in the telescope ; and though I had drawn up instructions to guide him in case he should be pressed for time, I felt it needless to give them. He observed all through the Eclipse with the polariscope eye-piece.

The first impression of the Moon on the Sun's limb was noted at 8^h 15^m 38^s·5 by BARRAUD, = 6^h 2^m 37^s·86 sidereal time ; this Captain BRAN-FILL thought too late, and it will be seen that my time was 25^s·2 earlier. After noting a few transits of the cusps for me, he returned to his telescope, and watched the progress of the obscuration. He says, " The mountainous ragged edge of the Moon's apparent upper limb was very clearly projected on the Sun. When about three-quarters of the Sun's diameter (by estimation) was obscured I observed faintly luminous lines beyond the cusps and about half-way between the limbs of the Sun and Moon prolonged." I get the approximate time from another part of his notes as 21^h 4^m, and a copy of a drawing which I made to scale, and of which he approved is among the illustrations. " These lines were also seen by Major HEARN,* whom I requested to note what he saw. They had disappeared ten minutes after ; I did not make out the limb of the Moon, either near the cusps or elsewhere, till about five minutes before totality, and then only the apparent left (that is, true south) limb of the

---

* Major HEARN, of the Madras Police, was passing through Guntoor on duty.

Moon." A drawing to scale is given endeavouring to depict this. "I failed to see the entire limb of the Moon before totality. I noticed the cusp I was watching (the apparent left) break into beads and short lines of light, and suddenly, with the palest dark glass on, caught sight of a group of red prominences. On removing the dark glass, thinking the totality had begun, I was dazzled with the remaining sunlight. A moment* afterwards the totality had commenced.

"Immediately after the commencement of totality my attention was caught by a tall, narrow, brilliantly-lighted, rose-coloured, horn-like protuberance. With the Nicol and crossed quartz in, and the largest shifting diaphragm, I turned the centre of the small field " (8¼' diameter) "on this ; I received a very vivid impression of the beautifully clear features and colour of this protuberance. The background gave SAVART's bands, but the horn did not. With the finder I then sought the brightest part of the corona, and directed the instrument upon it (viz. the left upper quarter), when the first-mentioned group of protuberances was just disappearing" (the photographs show that this was about two minutes after the disappearance of the Sun); "this also was near where the line of dark spots had disappeared."† "I found this part clearly polarized in a plane passing through the Sun's centre. I determined the position by a reading of the graduated arc on the eye-piece tube taken when a wire in the eye-piece was a tangent to the Moon's limb at the spot."

I find the following statements in other parts of the notes :—"Bright white centre band at 119°. Bands disappeared at 180° and 92°. Wire a tangent to the Moon's limb at 52°." The plane of polarization would thus have been at 136°‡ and the radius of the Moon at 142°. I find from a projection that the position of this point of the Moon's limb at the Sun's centre would have been 141° two minutes after the Sun's disappearance, and it would have been less earlier. "When the central band disappeared,"

---

* Some doubts as to the intervals led me to refer to Captain BRANFILL about this portion of the description. He says that he used the word "moment" rather as meaning a short period than in its more strict sense, and he estimates the interval from the cusps breaking into beads up to the disappearance of the Sun as half a minute.

† The group of spots on the Sun's disk which with a low power appeared to be three, of which the middle one (noted by me as two) was largest.

‡ The plane of the wire was nearly in the meridian when the index read 0°.

faint bands were seen on the edge of the field right and left ; it appeared as if no plane could be found in which there was an entire absence of bands. The white centre band was clearly marked when the wire was perpendicular to the Sun's [Moon's ?] limb, and as clearly disappeared when turned about 45° each way." "The bands appeared on the Moon's disk very faintly."

This last phenomenon I did not understand, and at first it struck me that it might be from the interposed cloud; but Captain Branfill could give no information as to the central band ; he had not noticed a change from white to black, but the bands were very faint. I have since found that the eye-piece even shows the fringes carried over the edge of the limiting diaphragm, owing, I presume, to dispersed light ; and, of course, they would be similarly seen to cross the dark disk of the Moon.

" The double-image prism with two diaphragms gave the same result — plentiful polarization in the plane passing through the Sun's centre."

" When quite satisfied as to the polarized light in the corona, and its plane ' of polarization,' by repeated examination in various places ; I gave all my attention to the horn-like protuberance which was still clear and high. I used the smallest diaphragm and the Nicol with and without the crossed quartz ; and also the double image with the largest diaphragm ; but could not detect any trace of polarized light in it, any bands, or any changes of colour or relative brilliancy." — " I was still examining the same protuberance, and about to try the simple Nicol again when the Sun reappeared (much before time I thought) and put a stop to the observations ; for, on putting on a dark glass I lost sight of the prominences and all traces of polarized light."

I now revert to Captain Branfill's description of the tall protuberance on which it must be remembered that he was only using a power of 30. " The tall rose-coloured protuberance was the only one most carefully examined ; the tint with no dark glass, as well as with the palest, through which it was seen a little before totality, was a beautiful bright rose pink, with veins of silver light. The definition was very good, the outline clear, but irregular ; a detached cloud of the same tint, with a distinct gap between, hung over the top. The tint was slightly deeper here and there on the body of the protuberance, and curved silver-lined streaks pervaded it generally in the direction of its length or height. Near the centre and lower part there appeared to be a rent, or place of no colour, like a small opening or hole in a cloud."

"After totality, while watching the progress of the eclipse, I noticed two mountain-like projections which eventually proved to be very near the point of last contact, and I was able to note the time of their disappearance nearly ten seconds after the Sun's limb appeared a perfect curve, except the two notches left by these projections." Captain BRANFILL noted the curve of the limb generally perfect at $10^h 59^m 56^s\cdot8$ by BARRAUD, $= 8^h 47^m 22^s\cdot9$ sidereal time, and the disappearance of the mountains $8^s\cdot6$ later.

I find I have omitted to notice that Captain BRANFILL describes having observed before totality the usual blunting of the cusps, as though by cutting off the points ; a phenomenon of whose existence he was not previously aware. He describes the light when he looked outside the tent, when it was failing (some six or seven minutes before totality), as grey with a slightly yellowish tinge ; and the general effect as that of an approaching tropical storm without its sultriness. His account closes with the following remarks :—" I am surprised to find that I was so little excited or put off by what has been called the appalling spectacle of a total eclipse. Before the eclipse I was trembling with anxiety for the result; but the rapidly diminishing light warned me of the necessity of confining my attention to the work in hand, and, except a little haste at first to see and note all I could, I forgot the spectacle, and was as calm as usual."—" What alone did strike me with surprise was the sudden first appearance of the rose-coloured protuberances and their beautifully distinct colour and form, and the amazing height of the horn-like protuberance and its structure."

Captain BRANFILL left me two or three days after the eclipse, having to meet a steamer at Masulipatam.

Fifth.

The Silver-Glass Reflector and the Photographic Operations.

The instrument employed for photography was a silver-glass reflector of 9 inches clear aperture ; the speculum by Mr. With, of Hereford, and the mounting by Mr. Browning. It was determined to adopt the Newtonian form and to place the sensitive plates at the side of the tube, in order to find room, which would be very difficult at the mouth of the tube ; the small mirror thus rendered necessary was made unusually large, in order that it might reflect all the rays from a surface of some diameter ; and it was hoped that by this means, and by giving a sufficient exposure, a picture of the Corona might be secured. The light clouds so decreased the actinic power of the light as to defeat this, but still we have traces of the Corona. The mounting was designed for the low latitude of my station, and to combine efficiency with moderate cost ; and I think it creditable to the maker. The instrument was very firm and steady, while the force required to direct the telescope was very small. The photographic arrangements were very good and convenient. Some little improvements have occurred to me, but it was hardly to be expected that such would not be required in any instrument ; far less should we be surprised when it is not only an entirely new design, but, from the necessities of its construction, could not be practically tried before being sent to its destination. When I first saw the complete instrument in Calcutta—(it was in a very unfinished state when I left England)— there were a few little matters which I thought needed change, and these were attended to ; the only matter of real importance was the cutting of the base of the cast-iron pillar so as to allow the clock-weight to pass through. I am not sure that the other changes were improvements, except an alteration in the mode of setting the telescope in right ascension. The telescope was driven by a clock, which it was intended should be similar to that employed for Mr. De La Rue's 13-inch equatoreal ; the new conditions, however, involved changes, and though the original clock is very efficient, this was not so. It caused me a very great deal of trouble with a very unsatisfactory result. It is only fair to say that Mr. BROWNING had never made such a clock before. When the pattern of clock was decided on, I and Mr. DE LA RUE (whose advice in a matter so especially his own province as photographic arrangements was of the greatest aid to me) fully expected that the instrument would be ready in time to try the clock and remedy its possible defects. As it was, the clock was only in hand early in January, and it could hardly have been tried at all.

To return to the more especial photographic arrangements. The small (flat) speculum had a minor axis of 3 inches across, and the tube to carry the eye-pieces was 3⅜ inches in diameter. On to this screwed the frame, into which the dark slides slipped. This frame carried two wires at right angles to each other,* which were intended to be used as the wires in Mr. DE LA RUE's arrangement in 1860, but those were in the common focus of the object-glass and enlarging lens, and were magnified with the focal image. Here no enlargement was intended, and they were placed as near as possible to the surface of the sensitive plate. There were six dark slides for glass plates, 4 in. × 4 in., all fitting into the same place. They were entirely of brass, except that the corners on which the plates were to rest were of silver; of course, both for lightness, and to avoid increasing the distance of the wires from the sensitive plate, the sheet metal was very thin. These answered extremely well; the fitting was very good, and they worked with hardly a difficulty. The arrangement cost much thought and trouble, and the only mistake in it was, that there was no means of defining the position of the wires with respect to the axis of the telescope; and that they could not, therefore, be taken off with their frame, so as to allow ordinary eye-pieces to be used with their adapter. If they were removed, they could not be returned to the same position. A minor defect was, that the only means of adjusting their inclination to the meridian of the field, was by turning the telescope bodily in its collars.

The iron pillar of this instrument stood on a brick one capped with stone, precisely similar to what has been described for the Sheepshanks' telescope, save that to allow the clock-weight to pass down, a cast-iron pipe, 12 inches in diameter, and closed at the bottom, was sunk, and, of course, its upper end partly imbedded in the pillar. The tent was similar

---

* These wires were necessarily a little within the focus of the mirror, hence their shadows were affected with diffraction.

to that covering the Sheepshanks' instrument, save that it was 12 feet in diameter, and, as in that case, a waterproof sheet was an additional protection. The dark tent was 12 ft. × 6 ft., a strong wooden frame braced with hoop iron, and covered with cotton cloth and felt, and as a further security against light (for we had to make experiments in the day), country blankets covered it. There was a curtain capable of dividing it into two parts, one of which was used for preparing the plates, and the other for developing them, but practically the curtain was not used, though the practice of separating the operations was. The whole was made, and put up, by Sergeant PHILLIPS with assistance from the two Sappers.

When the instrument was up and adjusted a commencement was made of taking photographs of the Moon. The two Sappers (whom I had chosen on a report that they were competent photographers) had very much to learn. We had the usual troubles from want of cleanliness, and the usual difficulty in producing conviction that a mere appearance of it was not enough. The nitrate of silver had been fused by myself in Mr. DE LA RUE's laboratory, but when all other difficulties had been overcome, it seemed as though a bath made after his formula would not give clean pictures without a very minute portion of nitric acid. Several baths were made with different batches of distilled water, and with special precautions, still with the same result. I still believe the water was in fault, but we had but little time for experiments, and very reluctantly I allowed the minute quantity of nitric acid needed to be added to all the baths we were to use. Still the pictures lacked definition, and though I knew the clock was not going well, I was satisfied that the focussing was wrong. The ground glass was useless for this purpose, except as a rough guide, and I found that the only way to focus on the collodion surface was by noting small specks and dust in it, and then bringing the image into the same plane as the collodion, by close attention to the relative parallax of the spots and the lunar image. On the 11th August at $17^h 5^m$ A.M., I obtained the first satisfactory lunar photograph, and it was the only one, for mist and filmy clouds prevented any more being taken with moderate exposure till the Moon had waned far. The clock all this time had been giving trouble. I had tried everything short of taking it down and remounting it entirely, but without effect.

If the pendulum were allowed to make 70 or more revolutions per minute, it would go, and not very unsteadily, but its proper allowance was 60. Besides, the Siemens governor acted by jerks and only deranged the going. I now took down the whole clock; every part was cleaned and fresh oiled, and in putting it up again I was particularly careful to give as little play to the wheels as was consistent with freedom wherever there was any room for adjustment. The axis of the pendulum was made vertical, and the plane on which the brush acted was made carefully perpendicular to it; but, after all, I found that the only result I had got was that it was a little better than before. I now prevented the Siemens governor from acting, and that, as I expected, was an improvement. The ball of the pendulum was still (as it had always been) incapable of controlling the rate, and it was only by repeated delicate manipulations that I persuaded the brush to produce such an amount of friction as gave the right average rate, still it was fluctuating, and liable to stop at any time; indeed, during the total phase it did stop, though no great evil resulted, as Sergeant Phillips had, with great forethought, placed a man to start it again if it played tricks.

A system of regular drill was now commenced, so that each man might know his work. At first this was experimental only, having for its object to discover the time necessary for the series of operations, then I drafted the instructions given in the Appendix, and practice was regularly taken up. While all this was in progress I proceeded to observe transits of the Sun over the wires of the instrument, in order to obtain their positions, and I availed myself of the opportunity to lay down the spots visible. The process was as follows. There was one dark slide especially adapted for focussing, which was put into position, carrying the focussing plate: then a pasteboard stop was inserted in the tube, having an aperture such that the light which passed round the flat mirror was equivalent to that through an object-glass of $2\frac{1}{4}$ inches diameter. The transits were taken with the naked eye. I tried an eyepiece for magnifying, but it would not carry a dark glass, and the glare was, of course, intolerable. In any case, the position of the telescope in its collars convenient for work, was not so for the use of an eye-piece.

On the 12th August, I took 7 sets of transits of the Sun over the wires between $20^{h} \ 35^{m}$ and $22^{h} \ 32^{m}$ to detect any possible correction to the positions due to hour-angle. I found none sensible. The following small Table gives the inclinations of the wires to the parallel of declination, + being measured from west towards the north. The wire B was unfortunately broken on the evening of August 16, and A only appears on two of the plates. The inclinations observed were

On August 11 by 7 sets	A	− 39 15′·3		B	+ 50 32′·0	
12	5	− 39 14·0			+ 50 13·8	
14	5	− 39 3·1			+ 50 25·2	
16	3	− 39 57·2			+ 50 23·9	
Mean values of	A	− 39 15·8		B	+ 50 21·6	

On the same days the positions were observed of a large spot which was crossing the disk.

On August 11	21ʰ 22ᵐ	it was	0·4522 S. and 0·1847	following the centre.	
12	21 26		0·6151 S.	0·0219	,,
14	21 48		0·5101 S.	0·3779	preceding the centre.
16	29 40		0·3807 S.	0·4891	,,

On August 16, also, there was a group of spots two of which were close to each other, and appeared as one to the eye (these are the pair I saw simultaneously on the Moon's limb), I observed these two as one

On August 16   29ʰ 40ᵐ   it was   0·6649 S. and 0·6289 following the centre:

the foregoing measures all in parts of the semi-diameter.

It was arranged that Mr. W. F. Grahame, of the Madras Civil Service, should note the times of exposure during the Eclipse. He accordingly took a place in the Observatory tent, and during the progress of obscuration the drill of exposing plates and noting times was gone through; Mr. Grahame giving a short warning from the watch when the pre-arranged intervals (one minute each except the last) had nearly expired. The first warning, of course, was only for looking out; but Sergeant Phillips seems to have misunderstood it, and did not wait * till the Sun had actually been hidden (he estimated the sunlight to last one second after the exposure), but this was the only hitch. It is quite evident from the

---

* That was his statement, but I am satisfied the Sun was not visible, though some brightness was.

DRAWING BY M^R, J.O.N.JAMES,
SHOWING THE GREAT HORN,
FROM PHOTOGRAPH N° 1.

[BLACK REPRESENTING LIGHT]

appearance of the plate that there was some bright glare of light, but this in some measure renders it more interesting. The long interval before the last plate could be developed allowed the nitrate solution to concentrate, and eat off the iodide of silver in patches on the last two plates; and there are some stains, but fortunately these do not interfere with the practical value of the plates. When I first looked at the negatives I feared our labour was lost, but the more I examine them the more satisfied I am. I shall describe them from views with a Ross Microscope * with a 3-inch object-glass and an A eye-piece. The prints† will but faintly represent this, but they are from negatives which have been the result of two processes of copying. A far better idea of the originals can be obtained from the very beautiful drawings by Mr. J. O. N. JAMES, of the Surveyor-General's Office, which seem to me very perfect, but in which I may mention light is represented by darkness. They were made from the microscope: first a faint outline was made with a 1-inch objective and the A eye-piece, by means of the camera lucida, and then the whole was drawn from a direct view with the 3-inch objective. I have occasionally drawn Mr. JAMES's attention to defects of representation, or over-definition; but, on the whole, the drawings may be considered as the work of a conscientious copyist devoid of all theories.

Photograph No. I.

This was taken at 9ʰ 29ᵐ 51·5 by BARRAUD, = 7ʰ 17ᵐ 2·9 sidereal time. The exposure was as short as possible, probably less than a second. In this photograph some glare has fogged the plate a little, but the following things are noteworthy. 1st. The enormous horn on the north side, whose height as derived from the Moon's diameter (about 34 minutes) is 3′ 18″, corresponding at the distance of the Sun to 88,900 miles.‡ 2nd. The ridge of light extending round the apparent upper limb of the Moon, so bright as to be markedly seen through the thickest

---

* Lent to me by Messrs. BARHAM, HILL, and Co. of Calcutta.

† This refers to the paper prints originally sent. Mr. DE LA RUE has kindly superintended the engravings which illustrate this paper. [The paper prints were not sufficiently distinct to be copied, recourse has therefore been had to the glass positives mentioned at p. 7. W. D. L. R.]

‡ The boundaries, and consequently the height, would be increased by using some of the subsequent pictures.

of the fog, though the glorious horn is paled. Near the horn this light is clearly broken into beads, as may be seen in Mr. James's picture of the horn, and is occasionally double. 3rd. At its southern end this ridge is terminated by a protuberance of singularly complicated structure. Outside the luminous ridge I see traces in the microscope of another faintly luminous stratum. This, and the apparent reduplication of the image of the southern protuberance, at first made me fancy that there had been a telescopic tremor. A micrometer in the eye-piece of the microscope was used, therefore, to examine the protuberances, and I found that the positions and distances of the parts did not exactly correspond; I also find on close examination, that a prominence seen in No. 2 is on this faint stratum, and that there is no other trace of it in No. 1. Lastly, the image of the wire is double; this could not have been from movement of the telescope; besides the phenomenon was always visible with this wire during transits of the Sun. When examining *Antares*, on the only evening I had for using this telescope, I fancied I saw a reduplication of its image when out of focus, certainly (though the vision was not good) I saw none when it was in focus, nor did I spontaneously see the same phenomenon with *Saturn*, though when I searched for it I fancied I saw a trace. When focussing the Moon I always found the limb, cusps, and detached points of light single, and that with the large speculum resting very much as it would do when the telescope was in the position seen in Plate 4. In Photograph No. 6, where is much detail, there is no semblance of reduplication. The reduplication of the image of the wire is evidently therefore an effect of diffraction* on account of its being slightly within the focus of the mirror.

Photograph No. 2.

This plate was exposed at 9^h 30^m $49^s\cdot75$ by Barraud, $= 7^h$ 18^m $1^s\cdot4$ sidereal time, and the exposure lasted five seconds. North of the Great Horn we see a peculiar and faint figure (it is, I regret to say, nearly lost in the paper prints) shaped generally like a bow, but with interruptions and nuclei of light, and having an arrow-like spike in the middle of its base. It resembles Mr. De La Rue's c and r together, and has the spike in addition. Next we have the Great Horn, which is here much over-exposed. The Moon's limb has advanced as far as the point where the

---

* See Addendum B, page 46.

DRAWING BY Mʳ J.O.N. JAMES,

SHOWING THE GREAT HO↑

FROM PHOTOGRAPH №2.

[BLACK REPRESENTING LICHT

DRAWING BY Mᴿ. J. O. N. JAMES.

SHOWING THE GREAT HORN,

AS SEEN IN A MICROSCOPE FROM PHOTOGRAPH Nº 4.

BLACK ·· ·· ·· ·· ·· LIGHT

two lower branches seen in No. 1 meet, leaving only a trace of the bifurca-
tion, and the upper part of the Horn is of course larger than in No. 1,
as fainter parts have come into view. When this photograph is well
illuminated, traces of the spiral structure, so apparent in the rest, are
seen ; but it would be difficult to recognise it without the other pictures.
Passing on, the Moon's limb is on the edge of the faintly luminous stratum
I have described in No. 1, which of course is now far more marked ; and
as we approach the S. we see the prominence mentioned under No. 1 as
being in the faint stratum, and then reach the upper part of the former
terminal prominence, where the long exposure has now blotted out all
traces of structure. The neighbourhood of both these prominences is
marked by light flaring into the Corona in irregularly curved lines, and
this corresponds to the part of the Corona which has been described by
Captain BRANFILL and others as most bright.

Photograph No. 3.

This was exposed at 9ʰ 31ᵐ 57ˢ by BARRAUD, or 7ʰ 19ᵐ 2ˢ·8 sidereal time,
and for ten seconds. It is evidently less affected by light than No. 2,
and was probably taken through a light cloud. Here the Great Horn
again claims attention ; its spiral structure is now clearly made out.
The outline of the Moon's disk is wanting till we reach the south terminal
protuberance of No. 1, which is now nearly hidden ; and in its neighbourhood we see again the flare of which I spoke in describing No. 2.

Photograph No. 4.

This was exposed at 9ʰ 32ᵐ 49ˢ by BARRAUD, = 7ʰ 20ᵐ 0ˢ·9 sidereal time,
and for five seconds. Nothing is seen but the Great Horn,
but that picture is of singular beauty. The continually varying intensity of the light and its markedly spiral structure are
the material points. In the margin is a copy of an enlargement
(reversed) of this Horn by photography alone, which shows this ;
and a larger drawing by Mr. JAMES will be found in the illustrations, which very perfectly represents the appearance; not
perhaps as seen at any one time, but as it exists in the Photographs, and
is brought out by varying the illumination.

Photograph No. 5.

This was taken by a short exposure at $9^h 33^m 52^s$ by BARRAUD, $= 7^h 21^m 4^{s\cdot}1$ sidereal time. The Great Horn is still conspicuous on the east side of the disk (I think, both in this and the two preceding paper prints, the borders of this horn have been encroached on by the silver deposit); and the outline of the Moon is marked round three-quarters of the circumference. The top of a prominence on the N.W. side of the limb is seen. It may be noted that in part of the circumference the action of light seems to have been reversed and the Moon to seem lighter than the Corona.

Photograph No. 6.

This plate was exposed for but a short time (like the 1st and 5th) at $9^h 35^m 22^s\cdot5$ by BARRAUD, $= 7^h 22^m 34^s\cdot8$ sidereal time. It is a picture as late as it was thought prudent to take it during the absence of the Sun. On the S.E. side, where the Corona was brightest, are traces of it; and the whole limb from N. to S.W. shows a trace of Corona and a series of beautiful protuberances, only one of which, however, is large. In the original it appears inflated, to me it resembles exactly one of the toy balloons for children in the shape of an animal; there is a mark as of an open mouth, the eye and the neck are marked, and the tail stands out stiffly behind. I mention these details because they complete the appearance of inflation by the resemblance they cause to what one has seen in that state. I would especially draw attention to the appearance as of a strong current of air (so to speak) blowing from north to south, and bending over and even detaching and carrying away the tops of prominences.

Throughout this paper I have spoken of myself as sharing in the Photography. I certainly exposed and developed a few plates, and generally superintended all that went on, and so far I was the superintendent of this department; but the trouble of endeavouring to break in new and unskilled hands, and of carrying out the details, fell on Sergeant Phillips; to whose steadiness and determination to succeed the result in this matter is mainly due. He was, moreover, most useful in other ways, for I could always rely on his care, and was thus enabled to avoid constant exposure to the Sun. Indirectly he has been the means, therefore, of facilitating my other work.

Sixth.

Results.

I have now only to say what I believe the new knowledge from this Expedition is.

First. The Corona is the atmosphere of the Sun not self-luminous, but shining by reflected light. It is evidenced both by the Spectroscope and Polariscope that this is the case, but there is one reservation to be made. The Polariscope has shown clearly that the light of the brightest part of the Corona is mainly reflected ; but, looking to the flare which is seen in Photographs No. 2 and 3, it seems impossible to doubt that in those places there must have been some inherent luminosity in the Corona ; unless indeed we consider the flare as a modified form of protuberance. It is, I think, now certain that luminous gas issues from what is more strictly the Sun, and I apprehend this flare to be some of this.

Secondly. The Great Horn certainly was composed of incandescent vapours, and probably all the brilliant protuberances are the same. In the Great Horn these vapours were hydrogen, sodium, and magnesium. It seems to me perfectly certain that the ignited hydrogen issued from the Sun itself, and that it carried up with it the light vapours of sodium and magnesium far above the level at which they would naturally lie ;

hydrogen naturally would be the very highest of the gaseous vapours, and consequently the coolest; if, however, it were set free at the surface of the Sun it would be intensely hot, and seek, with great violence, to ascend, in which process, if there be a stratum of heated vapours, such as is usually believed to exist round the Sun, the hydrogen would partly displace and partly carry up these vapours, and the lighter would be taken in preference. In fact, in this case it has carried the two lightest, and that of iron, which is so much heavier (I think we may presume this from the absence of the line corresponding to E), was either displaced or dropped sooner than the height at which I observed. Photograph No. 1 shows that there were two jets of vapour concerned in forming this Horn. One, the largest, and most northerly, is seen nearly perpendicularly to the limb, and seems also to have been the most luminous; the other issues about 20,000* miles towards the south and at an angle. They met at a height of some 16,000* miles, and the result was the rapid vorticose motion, which is evidenced in all the photographs as having existed in the upper portion. I believe I have the good fortune to be the first person to recognise such a phenomenon. In the fac-simile of Mr. De La Rue's Photograph No. 25, and in the enlarged and touched copies, there is evidently an appearance of a spiral structure in the floating cloud he calls C; but he does not seem to have recognised this, and his description of it is as "a cirrus cloud glowing with illumination." Captain Branfill, however, has described the spiral lines, and I recognise the same in the descriptions by Captain Tanner (in the *Asiatic Society's Journal*) and Professor Keru Luximon Chatrey, in a letter to the Director of Public Instruction at Bombay.† As to the other prominences, I think that gases or vapours issuing quietly from the solar surface would tend locally to raise the superincumbent ignited vapours. In places where they were most abundantly given out the elevation would be greatest, everywhere the gas would leak through in streams; producing occasionally such phenomena as the flare I have spoken of in Nos. 2 and 3. For a time the ignited vapour might, I think, form, as it were, a case for the light

---

* These dimensions refer to the projections on a plane perpendicular to the visual ray.

† These two gentlemen, I may mention, observed at Bijapoor in concert with Captain Haig, R.E.

included gas, which would be to all appearance inflated like the animal figure in No. 6. Soon, however, the slightly coherent casing would be burst and the gaseous contents would issue freely; the heavier vapours would, of course, to some extent be carried off by the gas, but would mainly settle down in small masses. Such, I think, is the state depicted in the southern protuberance of No. 1.

I would now draw attention to Plate No. 1, and the glare and luminous stratum. If that glare be from sunlight, it must, I think, be acknowledged that the remaining ray was but small. The luminous nearly even stratum then is not the Sun; but it is intensely bright; so much so, that nowhere is it lost in the solar glare. Its height is but small (I estimate it at 7,200 miles), and I believe it to be the mass of heavy luminous vapours, to whose elective absorption we owe the Fraunhofer lines in the Solar Spectrum. At the north end of this stratum near the Great Horn, it is broken into beads of light;* and I am disposed to think these are the veritable Baily's beads, of which I have always felt that the description would be difficult to apply to sunlight; I mean the statement which has been made of the light being silvery, &c. If these beads are really phenomena of the absorbing stratum, one can well understand the use of such terms. That will not, of course, apply to the elongation of planetary limbs in transits. It is true that not much of the details of these photographs has a sharply defined outline, but the picture of the Moon, taken on Aug. 11, shows that the focus was then perfect; and it was unchanged. Besides the fine markings here and there in No. 1 S. Protuberance, Nos. 2 and 3 Flare, &c., could hardly be seen if there were a sensible want of focussing, and I think one could hardly expect the surfaces of such masses as I have supposed these prominences to be, to have sharp definition under a high power. Captain Branfill's power was 30, which would have made the apparent diameter of the Moon 17°·0. If we take this in another form; and, to compare it with the photographs, consider what sized image would give this angle at the ordinary distance of vision (10 inches), we find the diameter would be 2·989 inches; now my original photographs are 0·75 inches, and very little definition is lost in their enlargement to 2¼ inches diameter. I do not think, then, that Captain

* This is the same place where Capt. Branfill saw beads (p. 25).

BRANFILL's account is irreconcilable with what I have taken from the photographs.

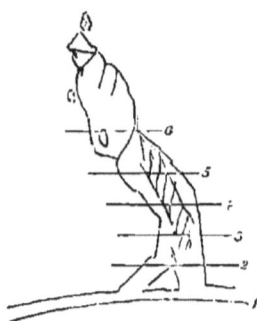

In the margin is a copy of an outline of the Great Horn, as drawn by myself with the camera lucida (roughly) from Photograph No. 1, aided somewhat by the others as to the boundaries of the top. On it the successive images have been superposed, and the bases showing the successive positions of the Moon's limb marked. A comparison of the spaces between these with the elapsed intervals between the photographs would, I think, prove conclusively, were any doubt existent, that the Horn was gradually covered up by the Moon. A similar process with the S. protuberance produces a like result, but the want of marks of reference makes the evidence less satisfactory.

The wire is only seen in Nos. 1 and 2 Photographs. Hence such an analysis of the results as is given in Mr. DE LA RUE's Report on the Eclipse of 1860 would be out of the question, and I hope that I have sufficient matter of value to make such an addition less missed. I find, however, from these photographs, by comparing the chord of the luminous arc with the wire, that the last visible point of the Sun's limb was 21° S. of the E. point of the Moon. I have found by calculations that the inclination of the Moon's apparent orbit was 16° to the parallel of declination. From these data I deduce that at nearest approach the Moon's centre was 6″·0 from the Sun's ; and that it passed to the north of it.* I have calculated the nearest approach from the *Nautical Almanac* data (but using 8″·93 as the mean solar parallax) by Professor CHAUVENET's formulæ, and find it 4″·0. I also deduce (using OUDEMANS' value for the Moon's semi-diameter in eclipses) that the total obscuration should have taken place one second before the exposure of the 1st plate, whence I think we may say that this phenomenon was 2 seconds late, if the longitude be the geodesical value. The duration of total phase by these formulæ and data should have been 5ᵐ 30ˢ·0 of mean time, whereas the interval between the first and last photographs is 5ᵐ 31ˢ.

* In Addendum C, p. 46, are given the results of a calculation, kindly made by Mr. HIND, of the circumstances of the eclipse at my station, using my determination of the latitude and longitude. (August, 1869.)

From Mr. Hind's chart I deduce that the duration at Bijapoor should have been 317^s; it was actually observed as 310^s. At Guntoor it should have been on the same authority (which is identical in result with my prediction) $5^m 45^s$; and if the error of duration was the same as at Bijapoor, for which I am indebted to the Hindoo Professor of whom I have before spoken, then the actual duration was $5^m 38^s$, and my last photograph was taken 8 seconds before the Sun's reappearance. It would appear also that the difference of the semi-diameters of the Sun and Moon was a mean between the values of the two used by Mr. Hind and myself in the last calculation.

I have now completed the narrative of my proceedings of all sorts. It was an anxious time to me, from the long delays which reduced the time available for preliminary arrangements at Guntoor, so that, in fact, not a fortnight was available for photographic practice, for one half of which the Moon would be low and pale. Nevertheless, I have I trust added somewhat to previous knowledge. If any one should think my theory of the protuberances not justified by the evidence produced, I will beg that judgment may be reserved till I send the original photographs. Several positive transparencies will be in England shortly, as they are to be taken by Sergeant Phillips. I have reserved the negatives to be sent by another opportunity,* when I have ascertained that they are not the only records of my work in this department.

J. F. TENNANT, Major R.E.
In charge of Eclipse Expedition.

Calcutta, October 24th, 1868.

---

* They are now deposited with the Astronomer Royal. (June 23, 1869.)

APPENDIX.

INSTRUCTIONS FOR SERGEANT PHILLIPS, R.E.

Commence at 20 minutes past 9 to prepare plates. The whole six must be selected carefully, cleaned, and marked, as well as the six Chassis. Three plates at least must be in the Observatory before totality begins, but there will be abundance of time (9 minutes), and it will be well to have all these and both Sappers ready.

The first plate is to be exposed as soon as the Sun vanishes, and the exposure will be about one second. After placing the Chassis in the slide (frame) in the telescope, lift the cover clear and about a quarter of an inch from the mouth of the tube. Hold it so for 2 or 3 seconds before removing it to expose. On removing it, call out " stop " or " open," as the case may be, as a signal to the recorder, who will note the time. Then, *before removing the chassis from its cell,* read off its number, which will be also recorded. After this, change as rapidly as you can, to be ready for the next exposure. You will have a full minute to each plate for all operations.

Be very careful to avoid over-development. Our negatives will be in some respects over-exposed if there be no haze, and will come out quickly. They should, too, be thin for enlargement.

ADDENDUM A.

Since writing and despatching this Paper I have heard of the proceedings of others and learnt some of their results.

It is clear from what others have seen that I may have been mistaken in the absolute identity of the yellow line, which I have called D, and ascribed to sodium, and the green line which I have identified with *b* seems not to have been seen since. By the same mail which brought me the last proofs of this paper, I learn that Mr. LOCKYER has, also in an exceptionally tall prominence, seen evidence both of sodium and barium, and as to the *b* line the existence of one in this neighbourhood is confirmed by Mr. JANSSEN, also at Guntoor, and M. STEPHAN, in Siam. When I looked at these lines on first closing the jaws of the Spectroscope slit the line C appeared single; that I have called D as if more sharpness would have made it double; and the *b* line like three run together. This progressive multiplication seemed to me a delusion, and before taking the second readings of solar dark lines, or attempting identification I had made up my mind that the dubious description best suited my impressions. When, however, I compared the readings I found that there might have been no delusion ; and as I think any one else would have done, identified the lines, though I did not think myself justified in altering my description, of which a note was shortly made to prevent change in it. It seems now not impossible that D and the usual line may jointly have been concerned in my impression of the line at 238 divisions on my scale.

Notice has been taken of my after identification of F. On examining the readings of the lines on p. 17, it will be seen that F was the last line of one set of readings and the first of the next ; in each case being near the limit of distinct vision. This circumstance drew my attention to its position and appearance on the day of the eclipse as on previous occasions when I had examined the lines. I was, therefore, in a position to say that from these marks the line I saw, and which I had some trouble in trying to connect with the scale, was very near F. When I found C was clearly seen the conclusion that my line was F, its companion in the hydrogen spectrum was so obvious as I think to justify the words I have used in p. 20.

I purpose now to make some remarks on the theory which I have ventured to put forward, and I begin with noting that the observations in Siam are, according to the Report I have seen, strongly confirmatory of my view of the Great Horn. The observer mentions that some of the lines extended over a part only of the length of the slit (width of spectrum) when it was in the direction of the Great Horn's length, and I deduced from the description that the lower part of the Horn showed most lines, a result which I had anticipated.

Accounts which have reached me of the opinions of some eminent men have led me to consider my Theory. I have heard of none similar, and what I have now to say is rather in explanation and amplification of the statement in the Paper than in modification. There is, I believe, a gaseous atmosphere to the Sun sufficiently dense to reflect the solar light. It seems to me that, though some portion of the Coronal phenomena may be terrestrial, yet the flare is not so; and the observations of polarization point to a very different angle of incidence on the reflecting particles from any that is consistent with reflection in the atmosphere. Indeed, where the line traversed by the ray is so nearly straight, the polarization if sensible would, I think, rather be that of a ray which has passed through a bundle of plates or at right angles to the plane in which both Captain Branfill's and Lieutenant Campbell's observations show that it is.

Hydrogen issuing from the solar surface would be intensely heated, and, I think, would be greatly condensed. In this state it would, were there no atmosphere, rapidly expand, absorb its heat, and become invisible, so that the existence of any visible prominence would become, I think, impossible; above all, it would be difficult to account for one of the enormous height of the Great Horn, and if that was really revolving and the dispersive effect of centrifugal force added to other causes, the difficulty is increased. But if there be a dense atmosphere, as I have supposed, then the resistance offered by it to the diffusion and expansion of the issuing gas would prevent its becoming instantaneously invisible. I think the gas would be constantly dissipating from the upper surface of Mr. LOCKYER's Chromosphere, and becoming invisible while it would be supplied from below. A prominence, then, whether enclosed in an envelope of vapour or no, would not be the whole extent of the hydrogen which is seen in it, but a form dependent on the relative amounts of supply and dissipation above and around for its outline and size, and within which the heat of the gas is enough to make it visible; of course this form would vary with every circumstance of supply and state of the solar atmosphere.

It is true this theory calls for an immense evolution of hydrogen, and both this and the destination of the gas must be settled before it can be finally accepted as true; but meanwhile it, I think, explains more than any I have seen, and may serve till some facts entirely inconsistent with it are found.

In closing this I wish to acknowledge the services, in the publication of the paper, of Mr. WARREN DE LA RUE, to whom I owe so much besides. To his zeal in a labour (I believe) of love are wholly due the enlarged engravings of the photographs, and I have to thank him generally for a superintendence which thus makes the distance at which I am an advantage to those who read these pages.

J. F. TENNANT, MAJOR R.E.

Mooltan, June 23, 1869.

ADDENDUM B.

I am indebted to Mr. DE LA RUE for the suggestion that diffraction is the cause of the re-duplication of wire A. This early occurred to me, and was at first laid aside because it appeared that it should also have doubled B, which was in contact with A, and also out of focus. I believe this is the true solution, however: a plane passing through B, and perpendicular to the collodion film, passed (when I was taking transits of the Sun) very nearly through the eye; thus the wire would be seen through the film. In the case of A this plane was far from the eye and I had only the effect of diffraction.

J. F. T.

Aug. 21, 1869.

ADDENDUM C.

GUNTOOR.

Longitude	80° 27′ 15″	East
Latitude	16° 17′ 29″	North
Middle of Eclipse, 1868, Aug. 17 ..	16ʰ 10ᵐ 53ˢ	M.T. at Greenwich
Sun's Semidiameter	15′ 50″·6	„
Moon's Apparent or Augmented Semidiameter ..	16′ 59″·1	„
Position Angle of first Internal Contact, or point when light first disappeared N. E. S. W.	105°	„
Position Angle of last Internal Contact, or point where light reappeared N. E. S. W.	287°	„

Relative Positions of Moon's Centre to Sun's Centre:

Aug. 17, 16ʰ 8ᵐ 0ˢ G.M.T. (beginning of central phase) ☾	20″ N.	4ˢ·5 W.
16 10 53 „ (greatest phase) ☾	1″ N.	0·1 W.
16 13 45 „ (ending of central phase) ☾	18″ S.	+ 4 E.
Nearest Approach of Centres ..	1″·3 N.W.	
Moon's Apparent Relative Hourly Motion in R.A.	23′ 27″·3 E.	
„ „ „ „ in Decl.	6 32·2 S.	
Moon's Apparent Declination	13° 3′ N.	
Orbital Angle	15° 58′	

ADDENDUM D.

An examination of the original negatives, in which the luminous prominences are depicted with great intensity and fine definition, has satisfied me that the want of distinctness of the lunar disc in relation to the background was unavoidable under the actual circumstances of the case. The possibility of bringing out the lunar disc depends on the actinic power of the corona surrounding it, at the time of observation ; but it will be recollected, not only that a haze covered the sky at Major TENNANT's station during totality, but that, on account of the extent of the eclipse, the Moon shut off the brightest part of the corona, except at the commencement and end of the total phase near the points of first and last internal contacts.

W. D. L. R.

October, 1869.

LIST OF ILLUSTRATIONS.

1. Plan of Mr. Wilson's House and Ground at Guntoor.

2. View by Sergeant Phillips, showing Observatories.

3. Drawings showing two Phases of the Obscuration.

4. Copy of a Photograph of Silver-glass Equatoreal.

5. Enlarged copies, Plates 5^a, 5^b, 5^c, 5^d, 5^e, 5^f, of the six Photographs.[*]

6. Drawings showing Horn of No. 1 Photograph (greatly enlarged).

7. Ditto showing Horn in No. 2 Photograph and the Bow-shaped Prominence.

8. Ditto showing the Horn as seen in No. 4 Photograph.

9. Copy of a Photograph of the Spectroscope.

10. Copy of a Photograph of the Polariscope Eye-piece.

---

[*] These copies have been made from the glass positives, in which the lunar disc is about 2½ inches in diameter (see page 7), which Major Tennant obtained directly from the original negatives by means of the enlarging camera. The mode of procedure was as follows :—In the first place, enlarged negatives on glass were procured, in which the Moon's disc is about 7·65 inches in diameter, and in which the luminous prominences are consequently on a scale sufficiently large to admit of being accurately traced. Positive paper prints were made from these negatives, and the centre of the lunar disc was found in them by a graphic method, and these portions of the lunar disc drawn in where it was necessary to do so in order to complete the circle. Tracings taken with great accuracy from the prints were then transferred to zinc plates and etched, so as to form six templates for use with the pantagraph. By means of one of Wagner's (Berlin) beautiful and accurate pantagraphs the outline was transferred on the steel plates by running the guide-point of that instrument in the etched groove of the zinc templates. The details were filled in mainly by reference to Major Tennant's glass positives, but before the final completion of the engravings, proofs were carefully corrected by comparison with the original negatives deposited in the Royal Observatory : this final operation was done in the presence of Mr. Airy, the Astronomer Royal, Admiral Manners, the President of the Society, and Mr. Stone, Secretary, who expressed themselves satisfied with the result. The stains and holes in the original photographs have not been copied ; moreover, the lunar disc has been made more distinct from the background[*] than it is in the original photographs ; lastly, although every care was taken to make the diameter of the lunar disc as accurate as possible, yet it cannot be considered as rigorously so, in consequence of its indistinctness in the photographs. As Major Tennant has distributed transparent copies to English and Foreign scientific bodies, and as the original negatives are now in the Greenwich Observatory, reference can always be made to them, whenever it is thought necessary to do so.—Warren De La Rue.

[*] See Addendum D, p. 47.

No. 2.

COPY OF A VIEW BY SERGEANT PHILLIPS, R.E SHOWING OBSERVATORY TENTS.

| Sheepshanks. | Silver-glass. | Dark Tent. |

No. 3.
DRAWING OF ECLIPSE, AT 21ʰ 4ᵐ M.T.

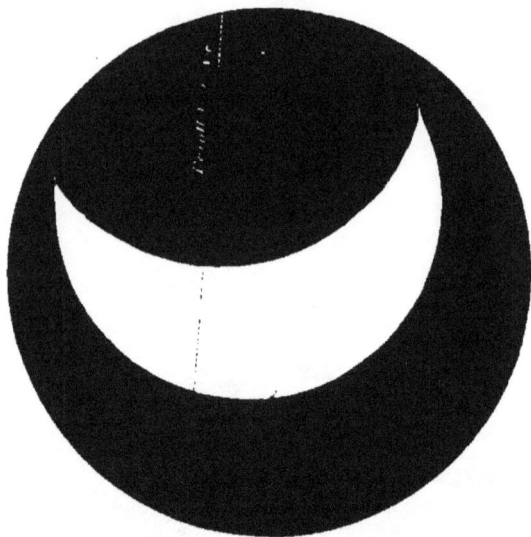

DRAWING OF ECLIPSE, AT 21ʰ 25ᵐ M.T.

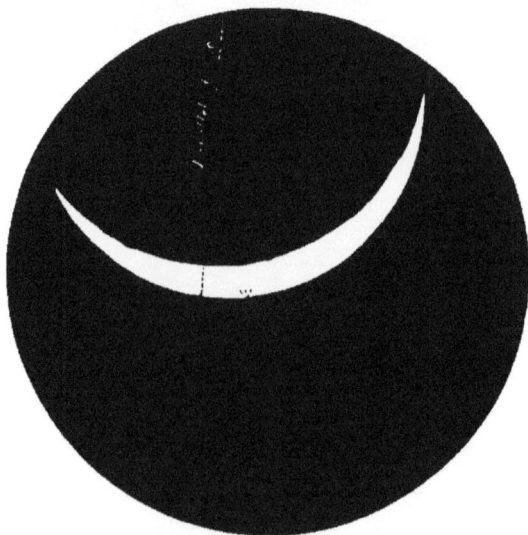

NOTE. - . in each figure marks the lowest point of disk.

No. 4.

Copy of a Photograph of the Silver-glass Equatoreal.

No. 9.

SPECTROSCOPE.

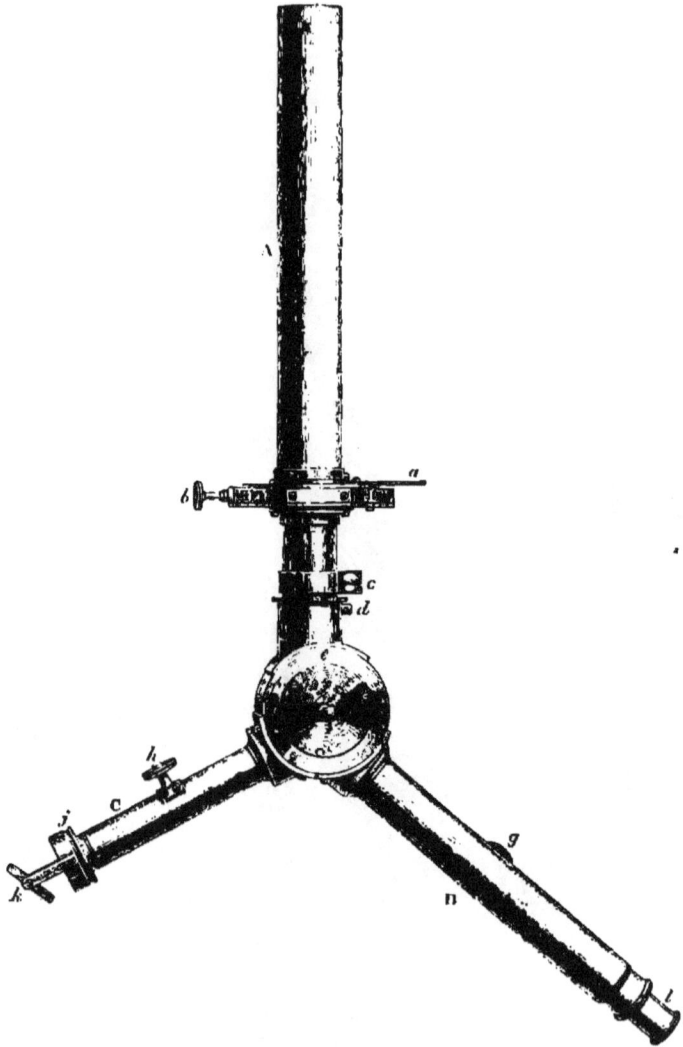

A is the Tube passing into the Telescope.

B. The Small Telescope for viewing the Spectrum.

C is the Collimator for showing the Scale.

a. The handle, by touching which the length of the slit is adjusted.

b. The screw for adjusting its width.

c. A captan-headed screw for binding the spring tube seen above it, and thus clamping the Instrument. The portion below the collar on which c acts is removable, and an eye-piece fits in by which the jaws of the slit can be seen, and the wires of the Finder made to coincide with them.

d is a small screw which has to be taken out before the collimating lens can be removed.

e is a cylindrical drum containing the prism (fastened to a plate, *f*), and carrying the tubes, and A, B, C, at the proper angles.

g is the milled head for focussing the Telescope B, and *l* is the eye-piece.

h is the milled head for making the Scale (placed in the cell, *j*) visible; *k* is the Mirror for reflecting light along C.

No. 10.

Polariscope.

A is the adapting tube for the Telescope, having the pointer or reading index.

a is the double image prism in position.

b is the rectangular slide, and

c the jacket, in which between *b* and *d* is the eye-piece.

d is one of the shifting diaphragms in position, close to it but lower down in the figure is the wire.

g g are the two smaller diaphragms of the same construction as *d*.

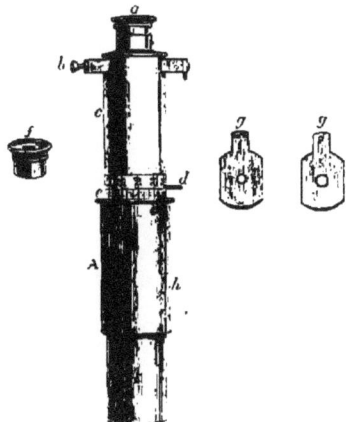

Exposed at 7^{h} 17^{m} $2 \cdot 9^{s}$ S 1
during 1 Second

Exposed at 7 18. 1·4. S 1

during 5 Seconds

Exposed at $\overset{H}{7}$ $\overset{M}{19}$ $\overset{S}{28}$ S T

during 10 Seconds

Exposed at 7 20. 09 S 1

during 5 Seconds

Exposed at 7. 22 3+8 S T
during 1 Second.

www.ingramcontent.com/pod-product-compliance
Lightning Source LLC
Chambersburg PA
CBHW020236090426
42735CB00010B/1720